WNBA Hot Ticket

SEATTLE STORM

JOSH ANDERSON

Lerner Publications ◆ Minneapolis

To Leo and Dane, the biggest superstars I've ever met.

The stats and information in this book are accurate through the 2024 WNBA season.

Copyright © 2026 by Lerner Publishing Group, Inc.

All rights reserved. International copyright secured. No part of this book may be reproduced, stored in a retrieval system, or transmitted in any form or by any means—electronic, mechanical, photocopying, recording, or otherwise—without the prior written permission of Lerner Publishing Group, Inc., except for the inclusion of brief quotations in an acknowledged review.

Lerner Publications Company
An imprint of Lerner Publishing Group, Inc.
241 First Avenue North
Minneapolis, MN 55401 USA

For reading levels and more information, look up this title at www.lernerbooks.com.

Main body text set in Aptifer Slab LT Pro / Typeface provided by Linotype AG

Library of Congress Cataloging-in-Publication Data

Names: Anderson, Josh, author.
Title: Seattle Storm / Josh Anderson.
Description: Minneapolis, MN : Lerner Publications, 2026. | Series: WNBA hot ticket (Lerner sports) | Includes bibliographical references and index. | Audience: Ages 7-11 | Audience: Grades 2-3 | Summary: "The Seattle Storm joined the WNBA in 2000 and won their first championship in 2004. Since then, the Storm have been one of the league's winningest teams. Discover the key to their success"—Provided by publisher.
Identifiers: LCCN 2024046223 (print) | LCCN 2024046224 (ebook) | ISBN 9798765670064 (library binding) | ISBN 9798765683576 (paperback) | ISBN 9798765681978 (epub)
Subjects: LCSH: Seattle Storm (Basketball team)—Juvenile literature. | Women's National Basketball Association—Juvenile literature.
Classification: LCC GV885.52.S295 .A534 2026 (print) | LCC GV885.52.S295 (ebook) | DDC 796.323/640979772—dc23/eng/20241224

LC record available at https://lccn.loc.gov/2024046223
LC ebook record available at https://lccn.loc.gov/2024046224

Manufactured in the United States of America
1 – CG – 7/15/25

TABLE OF CONTENTS

A PERFECT POSTSEASON **4**

FACTS AT A GLANCE **5**

CHAPTER 1
STORMING INTO SEATTLE **9**

CHAPTER 2
AMAZING PLAYERS **15**

CHAPTER 3
BACK TO THE FINALS **21**

CHAPTER 4
A TICKING CLOCK **27**

Glossary. 30
Learn More 31
Index 32

Alysha Clark dribbles to the basket during the 2020 Finals.

A PERFECT POSTSEASON

FACTS AT A GLANCE

- The **SEATTLE STORM** won their fourth Women's National Basketball Association (WNBA) title in 2020. They had a perfect 6–0 record in the playoffs that year.
- After making it to the playoffs for the first time in 2002, the Storm have only missed out on the playoffs **FOUR TIMES** since then.
- **JEWELL LOYD'S** 939 points during the 2023 season set a single-season WNBA record.
- The Storm are one of two active WNBA teams with **FOUR CHAMPIONSHIPS**.

In 2020, the Seattle Storm wanted to keep their winning streak alive and win the fourth title in team history. To do so, they would need to defeat the Las Vegas Aces once more in Game 3 of the WNBA Finals. A layup by the Aces' best player, A'ja Wilson, and a long three-pointer by Angel McCoughtry helped Las Vegas take a small lead early in the game. But each time the Aces threatened to build a bigger lead, former league Most Valuable Player (MVP) Breanna Stewart answered for the Storm.

When Las Vegas had an 11–2 lead, Stewart took a pass from Alysha Clark and scored with a layup. One minute later, Stewart made a beautiful dribble move to get away from her defender. She cut the Aces' lead to 13–8 with a jump shot from the free-throw line.

A few minutes later, Las Vegas had once again built a seven-point lead. Stewart answered with another jump shot from the same spot. Then, with just over a minute left in the first quarter, Stewart connected on a three-pointer to pull Seattle within two. Behind Stewart's 11 first-quarter points, the Storm managed to take a 23–21 lead. They never trailed again and won the WNBA title.

The Storm's victory completed a six-game winning streak. The team won all six of its playoff and Finals games. The 2020 title was the team's second with superstar Breanna Stewart. While Stewart has since left Seattle, the Storm continue to be one of the league's most exciting and successful teams.

Storm players and coaches celebrate the team's fourth WNBA title in 2020.

During her six seasons with the Storm, Breanna Stewart (*in yellow*) scored 3,723 points and grabbed 1,578 rebounds.

Seattle guard Sonja Henning looks for a teammate during a 2000 game against the Phoenix Mercury. Henning played for the Storm from 2000 until 2002.

CHAPTER 1

STORMING INTO SEATTLE

The Seattle Storm joined the league as an expansion team for the WNBA's fourth season in 2000. For nearly its entire history, the Storm have played their home games at Climate Pledge Arena in Seattle, Washington. Climate Pledge Arena was first called KeyArena.

The team's green-and-yellow colors come from the Seattle SuperSonics. The SuperSonics were a National Basketball Association team that shared KeyArena with the Storm. In 2008, the SuperSonics left Seattle for Oklahoma City, Oklahoma. The Storm's name comes from the weather in Seattle, which is often wet and stormy.

Former Storm coach Lin Dunn (*left*) also coached several college teams, the WNBA's Indiana Fever, and the USA Basketball Women's National Team. Dunn coached her teams to more than 500 total wins.

Like many expansion teams, the Storm struggled for their first couple of seasons. They lost more often than they won in 2000 and 2001. But in 2002, the Storm made the playoffs for the first time. They have only missed the playoffs four times since.

It didn't take long for the Storm to reach the very top of the WNBA. In 2004, the Storm won a tough WNBA Finals series against the Connecticut Sun. The Storm captured their first WNBA title in only their fifth season in the league. Starting with that 2004 championship, the Storm went 10 years without missing the playoffs and won another title in 2010.

Sue Bird (*center*) is one of the best point guards ever to play basketball.

Lauren Jackson (*left*) was the first pick in the 2001 WNBA Draft. She spent her entire career in Seattle and holds multiple team records, including most career rebounds and blocks.

The team owed much of its early success to a pair of stars who were among the very best to ever play basketball. Basketball Hall of Fame forward Lauren Jackson and 13-time All-Star Sue Bird played their entire careers in Seattle. Their skill and leadership were a big part of the team's success during their first 10 years. Bird played for the team for 19 seasons and is the WNBA's all-time leader in games played.

HOOPS SCOOP

In 2003, Lauren Jackson became the Storm's first WNBA MVP winner.

In addition to her two WNBA titles with the Storm, Breanna Stewart also won three Olympic gold medals as part of the US women's basketball team.

Superstar forward Breanna Stewart led the Storm to their two most recent titles in 2018 and 2020. Stewart signed with the New York Liberty ahead of the 2023 season. The Storm took a step back in their first season without her. After depending on her for so long, they had to find new ways to win.

New stars emerged to take Stewart's place. Six-time All-Star Jewell Loyd increased her scoring. The team signed Nneka Ogwumike, a former WNBA MVP and nine-time All-Star. Forward and center Ezi Magbegor developed into one of the top defenders in the league. In 2024, Seattle finished fifth in the WNBA standings.

A FORCE FOR CHANGE

In 2020, protests were happening around the United States. People were protesting violence against Black Americans by some police officers. Storm players and team officials discussed ways they could create change. They started Force4Change. As part of the program, the Storm support four main goals. They are voting, education and lawmaking, lifting up Black women, and supporting LGBTQIA+ and BIPOC communities. The team helps meet these goals by raising money with local partners.

Force4Change allows the Storm to make a difference off the court.

Sue Bird fires up the crowd during the 2022 WNBA playoffs. Bird retired from playing after the 2022 season.

CHAPTER 2
AMAZING PLAYERS

The Storm started playing in 2000, but it would be easy to look at the arrival of Sue Bird as Seattle's true beginning. The team picked Bird first overall in the 2002 WNBA Draft after her incredible career at the University of Connecticut (UConn). Bird had led UConn to national championships in 2000 and 2002.

She spent almost 20 years with the Storm before retiring in 2022. Bird was part of all four Storm championships and was an All-Star 13 times. In addition to finishing her career with the WNBA's most games and minutes played, Bird is the league's all-time assists leader with 3,234. She ranks third all-time with 724 steals, and eighth with 6,803 points scored in her career.

The Storm set a record when 18,000 fans celebrated Sue Bird's final home game on August 7, 2022.

Bird's teammate for much of her career was Australian forward and center Lauren Jackson. Jackson played all 12 of her WNBA seasons in Seattle. She won three MVP awards and was an All-Star seven times. Jackson was often among the league leaders in points, rebounds, and blocked shots. She helped lead the Storm to titles in 2004 and 2010 and finished her career ranked sixth all-time in blocks.

Lauren Jackson won six Women's National Basketball League championships in Australia and five Olympic medals with Australia's women's basketball team.

Four different coaches led the Storm to their four WNBA titles: Anne Donovan, Brian Agler, Dan Hughes, and Gary Kloppenburg. Agler, who led Seattle to the title in 2010, is the team's all-time leader in coaching wins. From 2008 to 2014, Agler led the Storm to 136 regular-season victories and six playoff appearances.

Like Bird and Jackson, Breanna Stewart was also chosen first overall in the WNBA Draft. Stewart joined the team in 2016 and made a big impact, leading the team to titles in 2018 and 2020. In 2018, she scored 742 points—more than any other player in the WNBA—and won the league MVP award. Stewart's career scoring average of 20.8 points per game ranks third all-time in the WNBA. In 2023, after six seasons with the Storm, Stewart joined the New York Liberty.

Brian Agler (*left*) led the Storm to the 2010 WNBA championship and won the WNBA Coach of the Year award.

Guard Jewell Loyd was yet another first overall pick for the Storm. After a successful college career at the University of Notre Dame, Loyd quickly became a key player for the Storm. She won the 2015 WNBA Rookie of the Year award.

Lloyd is a six-time All-Star and was a key member of two Storm title-winning teams. When Stewart left Seattle in 2023, Loyd took over as one of the team's top scorers. She raised her scoring average to 24.7 points per game in 2023, the most in the WNBA that season. Her 939 total points in 2023 were the most by a player in a single season in league history. Loyd left the Storm to join the Las Vegas Aces before the 2025 season.

With Loyd's departure, Ezi Magbegor, one of the WNBA's top young stars, will help lead the Storm into their next era of success. The Storm picked Magbegor, a forward and center, in the first round of the 2019 WNBA Draft. She increased her scoring in 2023 to 13.8 points per game. Magbegor finished second in the league in blocked shots in 2022, 2023, and 2024. Magbegor earned her first selection as a WNBA All-Star in 2023.

Australian center Ezi Magbegor (*left*) played pro basketball in her home country before joining the WNBA in 2020.

HOOPS SCOOP

Jewell Loyd (*pictured*) ranks in the top five in Storm history for points, rebounds, assists, and steals.

Breanna Stewart (*in green*) reaches for the rebound in a 2018 game against the Phoenix Mercury.

CHAPTER 3
BACK TO THE FINALS

The Storm's first WNBA title came in a close series with the Connecticut Sun. The Storm lost Game 1 of the 2004 Finals 68–64. That left Connecticut one win from the series victory.

Clinging to a 67–65 lead at the end of Game 2, the Storm could only watch as Sun forward Nykesha Sales launched a three-pointer with 3.1 seconds left. The shot would have ended the series in Connecticut's favor. But it hit the side of the backboard and bounced away as time ran out, giving Seattle the win. The Storm won their first title two nights later in a 74–60 victory. Betty Lennox was the star of the game with 23 points.

Storm players pose with the championship trophy after winning their first WNBA title in 2004.

The Storm looked to be in control of their 2018 playoff series against the Phoenix Mercury. Seattle won the first two games by the same score of 91–87. The wins put them one game from their first WNBA Finals since 2010. But the Storm fell in the next two games in Phoenix, setting up a deciding fifth game.

The Mercury scored the first eight points of Game 5 in Seattle. Other than a moment in the third quarter when the game was tied, Phoenix led the entire game and headed into the fourth quarter up 63–59. But the Storm looked different in the fourth quarter.

Guard Jordin Canada (*left*) finished her four seasons in Seattle with 808 points and 460 assists.

Sami Whitcomb (*left*) started her WNBA career in Seattle in 2017. After two seasons with the New York Liberty, she returned to the Storm in 2023.

Seattle began the quarter with a layup by Sami Whitcomb. Then a jump shot by Storm guard Jordin Canada tied the game 63–63. Moments later, a three-pointer by Canada put the Storm up 66–63, their first lead of the game.

The game remained close throughout most of the fourth. The Mercury tied the game with two free throws with just over four minutes to go. If Seattle was going to earn another trip to the WNBA Finals, they would need to play their best basketball of the season during the game's final minutes.

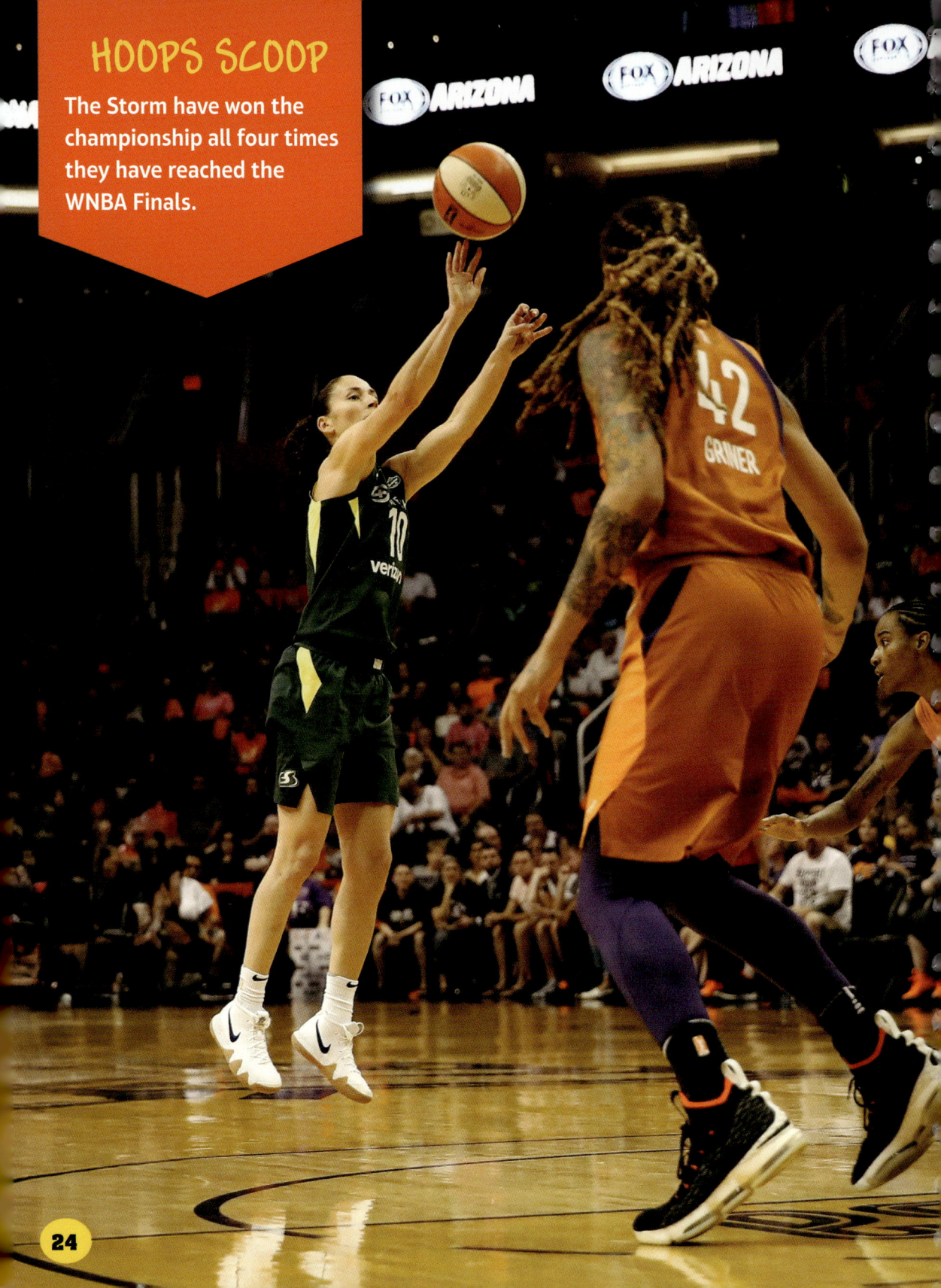

HOOPS SCOOP

The Storm have won the championship all four times they have reached the WNBA Finals.

Sue Bird brought the ball up the court. Breanna Stewart cruised toward the basket, and Bird threw her a pass. But Stewart came up short on the layup and missed. With three Phoenix defenders around her, Storm forward Natasha Howard somehow grabbed the rebound and fired it back out to Bird standing behind the three-point line. Without hesitation, Bird shot a three-pointer. It swished through the net.

Bird's basket gave Seattle a 79–76 lead, and they never trailed again. Their 94–84 victory put them in the Finals against the Washington Mystics. Eight days later, the Storm finished a three-game sweep of the Mystics for their third WNBA title.

Sue Bird (*center*) made 16 WNBA playoff appearances during her career with the Storm. She played in 60 playoff games and averaged 11.7 points and 6.1 assists per game.

Jewell Loyd ranks in the top 10 in multiple WNBA stats, including career points, steals, and minutes played.

CHAPTER 4
A TICKING CLOCK

The Storm are one of only two active teams to win four WNBA titles. Seattle fans have enjoyed so much success over the years that they have come to expect the team to win. That puts a lot of pressure on players and coaches to avoid losing seasons.

In 2024, Caitlin Clark, Angel Reese, and other great players joined the WNBA. Thanks to rookie superstars such as Clark and Reese, the league is more popular than ever. More people are watching the games and following their favorite stars. That puts even more pressure on the Storm to win.

Storm players, led by Jewell Loyd (*center left*), dance on the court before a 2024 game against the Minnesota Lynx.

Noelle Quinn took over as coach in 2021 and won her first playoff series in 2022. She aims to become the fifth coach in team history to lead the Storm to a title. A fifth title would make the Storm the most successful team in league history. But after superstar Stewart left the team, the Storm finished with only 11 wins in 2023. In 2024, the Storm more than doubled their wins with 25. They finished the season third in their conference and fifth in the WNBA.

While Seattle has one of the WNBA's top young players in Ezi Magbegor, 2023 first-round pick Jordan Horston is the only other young player who plays regularly for the Storm. The rest of the team is filled with talented veterans. They include Nneka Ogwumike and six-time All-Star Skylar Diggins-Smith.

With a team full of talented veterans, Seattle is ready to win now. The Minnesota Lynx are the only other active team with four WNBA titles. If the Storm want to win a fifth title before the Lynx do, they will need to do it soon while this skilled group is still able to play at the highest level.

Left to right: Skylar Diggins-Smith, Jordan Horston, and Nneka Ogwumike fire up their teammates before a 2024 game.

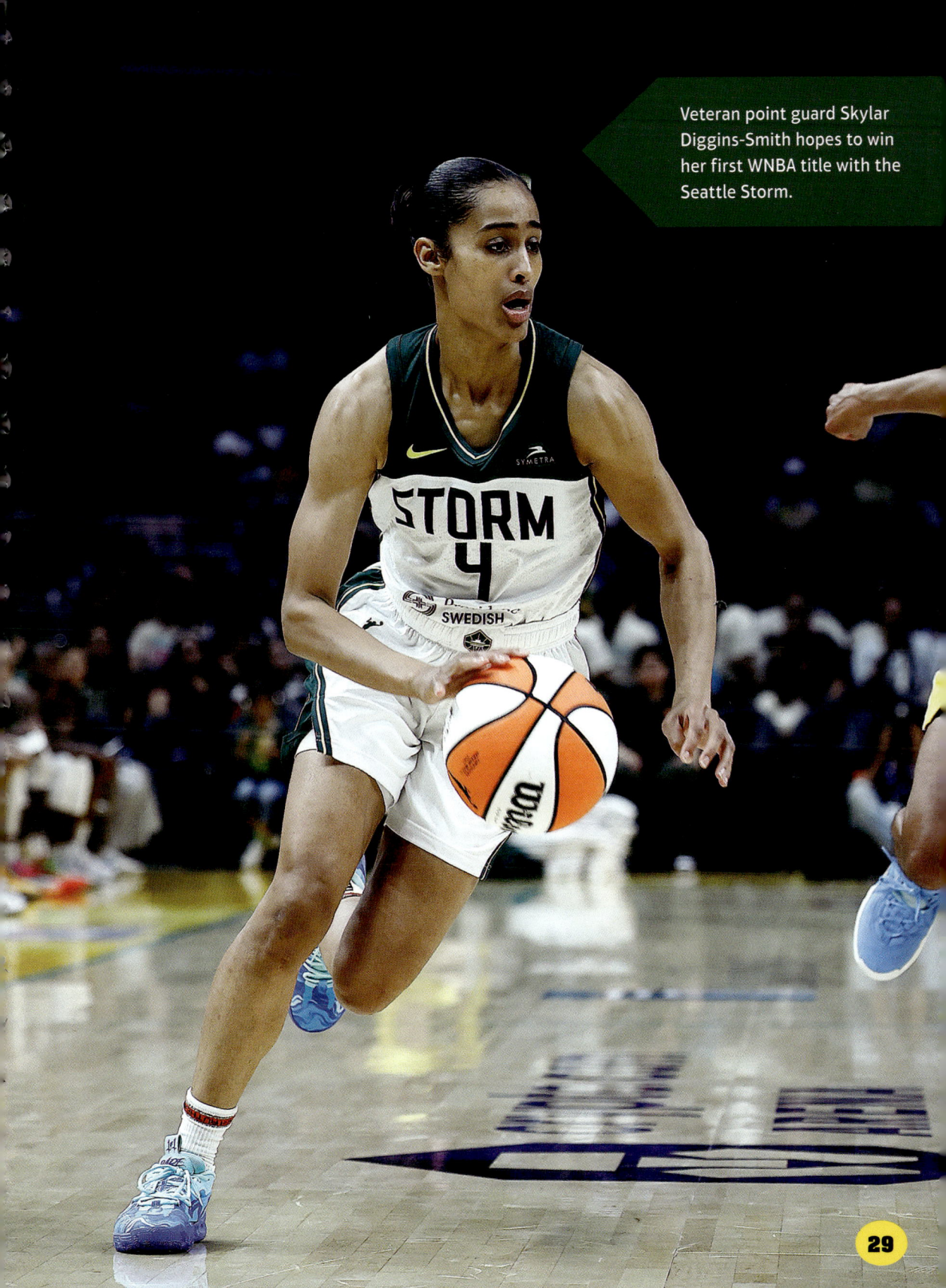

Veteran point guard Skylar Diggins-Smith hopes to win her first WNBA title with the Seattle Storm.

GLOSSARY

All-Star: a player chosen as one of the best in league to compete in a game against other top players

assist: a pass that leads directly to a basket

Basketball Hall of Fame: a museum in Springfield, Massachusetts, that honors the best basketball players, coaches, and team officials

draft: when teams take turns choosing new players

expansion team: a team that is added to an existing sports league

free throw: an open shot taken from behind a set line after a foul by an opponent

layup: a shot in basketball made from near the basket usually by playing the ball off the backboard

playoffs: games held after the season to determine each year's champion

title: championship

WNBA Finals: a series of games played to decide the WNBA champion

LEARN MORE

Ford, Jeanne Marie. *Breanna Stewart*. Lake Elmo, MN: Focus Readers, 2022.

Hill, Christina. *Sue Bird*. Minneapolis: Lerner Publications, 2022.

Seattle Storm
https://storm.wnba.com/

Whiting, Jim. *The Story of the Seattle Storm*. Mankato, MN: Creative Education and Creative Paperbacks, 2024.

WNBA
https://www.wnba.com/

Women's National Basketball Association Facts for Kids
https://kids.kiddle.co/Women%27s_National_Basketball_Association

INDEX

Agler, Brian, 17

Bird, Sue, 11, 15–17, 25

Clark, Alysha, 5
Climate Pledge Arena, 9
Connecticut Sun, 10, 21

Diggins-Smith, Skylar, 28
Donovan, Anne, 17

Jackson, Lauren, 11, 16–17

Las Vegas Aces, 5–6, 18
Loyd, Jewell, 5, 12, 18–19

Magbegor, Ezi, 12, 18, 28
McCoughtry, Angel, 5

Stewart, Breanna, 5–6, 12, 17–18, 25, 28

PHOTO ACKNOWLEDGMENTS

Image credits: Julio Aguilar/Getty Images, p.4; Julio Aguilar/Getty Images, p.6; Julio Aguilar/Getty Images, p.7; Otto Greule Jr/Hulton Archive/Getty Images, p.8; Otto Greule Jr/Allsport/Getty Images, p. 9; Otto Greule Jr/Getty Images, p.10; Chris Trotman/Getty Images, p.11; Abbie Parr/Getty Images, p.12; Steph Chambers/Getty Images, p.13; Ethan Miller/Getty Images, p.14; Steph Chambers/Getty Images, p.15; Christian Petersen/Getty Images, p.16; Tim Clayton/Corbis/Getty Images, p.17; Scott Taetsch/Getty Images, p.18; Sam Hodde/Getty Images, p.19; Christian Petersen/Getty Images, p.20; Otto Greule Jr/Getty Images, p.21; Justin Casterline/Getty Images, p.22; Abbie Parr/Getty Images, p.23; Christian Petersen/Getty Images, p.24; Christian Petersen/Getty Images, p.25; Ethan Miller/Getty Images, p.26; Steph Chambers/Getty Images, p.27; Steph Chambers/Getty Images, p.28; Ronald Martinez/Getty Images, p. 29

Cover image: Jeff Halstead/Icon Sportswire DNQ/Icon Sportswire/Newscom